Tales From the Heartland

Kerry Bashaw

Chapbook Press

Schuler Books
2660 28th Street SE
Grand Rapids, MI 49512
(616) 942-7330
www.schulerbooks.com

Tales from the Heartland

ISBN 13: 9781966196389

Library of Congress Control Number: 2025923739

Cover illustration: iStock.com/chainatp

Printed in the United States by Chapbook Press.

Dublin Fog

Far away in a mystic land where the hills are emerald green

Lies a village without a name that paints a pleasant scene

One fine day I found her there a forever Irish rose

She took my hand then showed me the way to where her garden grows

And she said

Come here rambler let me hold you tight

Let us be one all through the night

Clear your mind of all the bog

And feel my love in the Dublin fog

Like a flirting shadow in the dark her eyes enchanted me

Like a candle lit in the midnight hour her light surrounded me

No I couldn't deny the sweet caress that flowed from this dove I needed every word of my poetry to understand her love

I have her picture hanging on my favorite chamber wall

It brings me to a sweet surrender as the sun begins to fall

And now the spiral of the staircase will show me the way

Where the memory of my lady ends another day

Magical Night

Drink a cup from it's fountain for always it will allow

Find the eyes that sparkle hidden beneath a brow

See the fearless sunset kiss the field of green

Close the door of your nightmare and open freedoms dream

Unrestrained and freely is this eager child's kite

Wanting you to never let go throughout the magical night

Buffalo of the prairie roam wildly through it's soul

Sweeter than the hive is the sugar in it's bowl

Defiant is the fruit of all it's tameless lust

Savory is the filling bursting from it's crust

Touch these things than you and I will soon be taking flight

With total exhilaration throughout the magical night

Shudder with uncertainty and it will calm with a kiss

Tremble with anxiety and it will turn to bliss

Fever with frustration and it will end the chase

Hurry with impatience and it will slow the pace

It's a masquerade banquet a mystery in every bite

And deeply it will flow throughout the magical night

The Portrait

His eyes are cold and blue as the sea

And sober my thoughts that are mocking me

It has regrets that can't be undone

It looks for love from the ones who shun

A philosopher yes he had plenty of time

But instead caressing then spending every dime

Wrestling the fury of dreams too big

Accepting defeat for the game was rigged

His mind has knowledge in a simple way

But has sleeplessly tried to live for the day

He knows no touch of a loving hand

And his take on life is rather bland

It's not the age in his face he fears

But the wisdom learned each passing year

For each smile of laughter and tears he cried

Are splattered on the canvas and the paint has dried

The Legend of Unknown

It came from the night that abruptly had end

And from the darkness it's message transcend

It brought another day with seeds it had sown

It soon became the legend of unknown

It wandered freely with no direction home

Some days with friends some days alone

It never understood how far it had grown

Because that is the making of a legend of unknown

See how we mingle to and fro

But everyday we turn our heads slow

And gaze at the beauty that deeply is shown

We always wonder about the legend of unknown

Ivory Walls

He sought knowledge beyond a prison of doubt

He saw imaginative realms tossed about

He saw intriguing fascinations from intellect calls

For a book he found behind these ivory walls

She hungered for learning from a dream catcher's night

With heart mind and soul she brightened the light

Like a trumpet blast she heeded the call

To find a book beyond these ivory walls

The years go by with stunning ease

And yet the body will do as it please

If you see the world begin to sputter and stall

Look for a book beyond these ivory walls

Stir The Mist

The wizard sees all that is done

To his humble abode that is no longer fun

He wonders why the point has been missed

So now he must stir the mist

An incantation begins to swirl

The spell begins to curdle and twirl

The rain and valleys have patiently kissed

As the wizard of all stirs the mist

But low and behold the storm has ceased

And no longer growls an unwanted beast

The dawn is breaking from this iron-fist

Which is why the wizard stirred the mist

Travel Those Roads

I saw the eyes of a stoic wolf with the cunning of a fox

I saw waves of ivory glass crashed upon the rocks

I saw a wild dancer redeeming the young and the old

It was a gift that I found when I traveled those roads

I saw streams of chestnut light flow through her natural hair

A face so bold and strong with a skin so soft and fair

A trail of burning hearts rekindled from the cold

Immaculate wonder to travel those roads

I saw a castle of laughter among my fellow friends

And shook hands and smiles when it came to an end

Every casual memory will never crush or fold

For the serenity that I found as I traveled those roads

Song of Ghosts

Just past midnight with all their might

They float through the shadows their souls taking flight

You may not know them by the road they coast

But among the highway is the song of ghosts

You can hear them but you wonder why

They remain silent until they die

With sceptic thoughts you play their host

Try to listen to the song of ghosts

You see their visions at the rise of dawn

And see their innocence like a baby fawn

Please understand for they do not boast

And you will come to hear songs of ghosts

Layers of Green

Imagine a time and place I've known

Where love and beauty are shamelessly shown

Where eyes are open to nothing obscene

And of the layers of green, the layers of green

The comfort of shade from welcoming trees

A daily adventure the heart does seize

I pity the soul that has never seen

The layers of green, the layers of green

We say good-bye to the night at dawn

Creeping away from the glistening lawn

Please stop and look at a sight so keen

Oh the layers of green, the layers of green

Distant Thunder

Nocturnal cotton candy smear the turning globe

The neon tempest begins to blink and strobe

The crackling fire of a flash fire night

There is distant thunder coming tonight

The earthy smell of feline fur

Knowing and warm begin to purr

They perform their jig with free fall stroll

While the bells of distant thunder toll

Crack goes the light, boom goes the sound

Laying their song of shuddering pounds

Is it unsafe? You need not fret

It is distant thunder you can bet

Wetlands

Ker plop lands the frog on top

Of spongy moss and slop

The pools curdle and churn

In my eyes I long to learn

The trees bow on bended knee

And propose to swans who do not flee

Their feathers are lightly plucked

And not one of them is an ugly duck

The prince of the forest is somewhat near

With a royal gaze it knows no fear

I cannot recall such a playful scene

It is the foundation of nature's scheme

Calm at Midnight

The key slides from the ignition like a smooth leather glove

The wary engine cools without any push or shove

You begin to break away from the emerald city lights

Heading from the edge of the calm of midnight

You stroll into this pleasure lounge and flag a moonbeam down

Your tremors turn to peaceful joy as your head no longer pounds

The mystery and the romance become a poets delight

As you head into the darkness and the calm of midnight

The hum of the city coos a fading tune

The sounds of silence will be coming to you soon

No one can tell you anything they simply don't have the right

As you head into the calm, the calm of midnight

Heartland Woman

She is the sound of Michigan tides strolling down the hall

The smoothest looking lady at the masquerade ball

Call her by name with all your will

A whisper in your ear and your love will spill

Spanish dancers and mariachis are ringing in my head

While she smiles like a belle to everything I've said

Something in her eyes leaves me without doubt

If she loved me tonight it will turn me about

Heartland woman you are so innocently bold

With a freedom I wish I could hold

You sparkly like a diamond on a midnight beach

And you hold my love always within reach

The Total Package

A crow flutters cautious and alert

While the caretaker shovels in the dirt

The body below is lifeless and unmoved

"My friend I hate to tell you, you are worm food"

I lived my life without second sight

I need the total package tonight

He wanders down the street as the wind whips on by

His watery eyes see the sun in the sky

He sees his destination around the bend

A full plate and hearty smiles everyone's a friend

"I've struck a deal I don't have to fight"

I've been given the total package tonight

Her innocent embrace is a feather in the breeze

His little elf daughter age of three

The other kisses him his lover and friend

He holds this beauty with a love that has no end

He knows his job make others die with fright

But it reminds him of the total package he has tonight

Solace

He has come here tonight to sit beside the lake

His mind is warm and calm the coals have been raked

The mystery has decomposed solitude has filled the void

The vaults of senseless loss has now been destroyed

The face in the water may come to be unknown

But he lived his life like a rolling stone

The road behind him filled with beggars, thieves, and tramps

Removed his childhood fears of goblins, ghosts, and vamps

And passing time has made them forever never more

And he sees the truth in his modern lore

The lake lives on according to it's mother's vow

And the unshakeable truth is he is here and now

Whatever the task or challenge a fool can overcome

For a fool does not know when all is said and done

There is no need for pride, no need for regret

When simple is your hand, you have no need to bet

And the cards he played he let flutter away in the breeze

For the lake and him will live their lives with ease

Ebony Lover

I long to kiss that satin kiss

That Motown song could turn me to bliss

Philadelphia freedom that has no fear

This unchained melody is drawing me near

The soul of the Earth I can see it in those eyes

With pure Memphis passion that never dies

Ebony lover with rich dark skin

I wish no harm and long no sin

It is wrong to see you with possessive lust

For I long to love you and respect you I must

You are redemption with the touch of your hand

A colorful dove throughout the land

Fly Away

Each morning I awake under a welcome breeze

A falcon strong and bold peacefully at ease

The apple and the maple fill the open air

The time will pass on by without consent or care

I am a hungry hawk full of vigored youth

My eyes are full of questions like a novel sleuth

My past is soon forgotten and the present is my friend

The freedom of my flight is never going to end

I've waited for this moment ever since my birth

I'm now an eagle soaring high above the earth

When life gets tough I know just what I have to do

Take off with open wings and fly across big blue

A Taste of Freedom

Naive seagulls try to kiss the sky

Horizons melt where eyes have yet to pry

The wolfman idol has taken flight

While a chorus breaks the misty night

Have a taste of my freedom

Just open your eyes

Have a taste of my freedom

You won't need a disguise

Evening shadows begin to lurk and loom

Desolation is filled with a sweet perfume

Majestic timber bravely stand alone

And a voice is crying from somewhere unknown

A crystal world wrapped in a frozen shroud

Where each sliver of light shimmers through a cloud

The wind blows with always a breath to spare

As I hear a calling through the air

A Walk in the Rain

A little boy staying after school

Teacher caught him picking on Mary Lou

He knew when he got home that he would have to explain

Why he took so long to walk in the rain

Johnny was late getting to the dance

By the time he got there his girl had found new romance

The raindrops hid the tears he cried in vain

As he took a cleansing walk in the rain

The midnight hour is dark and cold

But I know all my love will unfold

And I know someday I'll board the homebound train

But for now I'll take a walk in the rain

Enough Time

We steal a moment every single day

So we know the night is never far away

The laughter we share becomes a knowing sigh

Although we say goodnight we never say goodbye

There are days when love is hanging in the air

And forgotten promises are no longer there

The love we need will never come too late

And we won't let go of our sweet precious fate

The headlights fade with patronizing glee

My solemn hand fumbles for the key

My heavy feet lumber down the hall

But the quilted net catches my fall

I'll always have enough time for you

Because I know what our love can do

Breath of Life

He skidded across the ice with all his might

Then claimed his victory in the snowball fight

The air is crisp and sharp as a knife

His lungs burn with the breath of life

She sits open minded taking notes

On all she has learned she never dotes

She sculpts each day for a better life

Her lungs are strong with the breath of life

I conclude this poem with this thought in mind

If you do not want to be left behind

Learn from all of your worthless strife

And fill your lungs with the breath of life

The Storyteller

Gather around your open minds
Turn on the lights, open your blinds
Her mouth is singing with throaty strength
Her prose is love at its glorious length

The strum of her guitar is a waterfall
High and mighty like an eagle call
But don't be afraid her song has might
Each note she plucks is a star at night

She is every woman bold and young
There is more to her than just her daughter and son
But the show is over and now it's clear
The storyteller has been here

Backyard Space

The gentle swish of the sprinkler head

The ticktock swaying in my canopy bed

The smell of autumn but not quite yet

The soothing ritual of another sunset

Critters and chatters of a nearby brook

The curious creatures that peek from a nook

In here is peace not the slogan kind

But real and tangible for a vivid mind

Oh how I wish this would never end

That my mind and this scene would forever blend

But my career now beckons yet I am not barred

For I know I'll return to my backyard

The Whisper

Her little man is tucked in snug bound for the morning train

He's dreaming of new frontiers on his way to memory lane

A familiar face he is wearing on his newborn baby's cheek

While she whispers a lullaby the kind we always seek

The evening rain and morning dew soothe the thirsty lawn

While they stare out the window at the calm consenting dawn

There was magic in the air for two lovers born anew

Their honest whisper strong embrace ushered their passion debut

The sobering lilies soothe the collective soul

The tears of sorrow shed as the bell begins to toll

One by one onto the tomb they silently emerge

As the whisper in the autumn wind calms the funeral dirge

Castles

Weary travelers are welcome here

Where knights errant melt their fear

The crack of laughter will soon commence

Until the days doldrums make no sense

The soothing fire that smokes and spits

Calms the mind from its childish fits

The maidens and princes dance their love

Without any shame from up above

The graying walls of the outside bricks

Plays with the mind and easily tricks

That the scene may appear full of doom

But inside the party is in full bloom

Sunset

The sky is now a dimming blue

My how the summer rapidly flew

It is nature's law in stone hard set

To end each day with a timely sunset

The day is given to every woman and man

Turning cynics and critics into enduring fans

Rays of red is a promise kept

That you will return to another sunset

Youth is king in its own way

And we shouldn't have it any other way

Wisdom is learned and soon well met

Cherish the beauty of another sunset

The Myth

He saw crystal visions while others were blind

On the food of knowledge he hungrily dined

His passion drove him from coast to coast

His dream was natural he need not boast

Geysers of plumage exploded about

His pirates bounty gave him some clout

Like an innocent child he kept looking around

In search of the myth with its mighty sound

Fortune and glory soon came his way

All he needed was to seize the day

His ship came in like others have scored

To hell all doubt and he climbed aboard

The Show

An old man spoke of a king he knew

Whose eyes were always a smiling blue

His mind was lucid and never dark as a crow

I wish I could have been there to see the show

She once told me of a woman so strong

That never backed down from anything wrong

Her heart was pure but with passion you know

I wish I could have been there to see the show

I stand here admiring the stones at my feet

Knowing that life will always repeat

Stories are told and legends all grow

I wish I could have been there to see the show

The Courtship

Two doors open and let loose the flow
Of a boy and girl their hearts aglow
They walk hand in hand with innocence in mind
To the woes of the world they are still blind

Yearbooks are signed and rings are exchanged
But in those two hearts nothing has changed
They have kisses of love as they enter their time
Now the ceremony has stopped on a dime

Two careers are steady but not for granted
They are grateful for all they have planted
Now he hopes she won't second guess
But with tears of joy she eagerly says ye

Friends

On a warm July they met one day

Both surprised to walk their way

For their music and styles reflected the same

Shaking hands they joined the game

Dreams became commerce they understood

They never let go of their brotherhood

With cheeky grins they toiled and rolled

Their camaraderie was never bought or sold

Slowly and quickly their lessons were learned

From each others path their worlds turned

It may be cliched to say all things end

But for miles and time they remember as friends